Coastal Images
East of Big Sur

Being colorblind gives an advantage when composing black & white... less confusion.

This special collection exhibits the lonely freedom of a hidden perspective selected from thousands of captures during years of travels. All images presented genuine without edits. Color sacrificed by proprietary process.

info@ BEACHNOISE.com
original fine art and custom work

0125

0351

0354

0430

0437

0471

0503

0531

0705

0780

0826

0920

0938

1085

1096

1173

1581

1608

1784

1976

2068

2180

2184

2294

2397

2467

2495

2607

2686

2688

2962

2969

3147

3151

3359

3621

3658

3714

3720

3795

3799

3916

3937

3943

4035

4036

4043

4070

4098

4099

4128

4193

4265

4533

4879

5171

5492

5541

5705

5750

5784

5811

5844

5846

6014

6095

6176

6209

6946

6990

7148

7339

7656

7693

7783

7939

8173

8345

8407

8470

8471

8766

8815

8889

8949

9024

9211

9297

9353

9430

9970

9975

9980

9992

9998

10002

www.ingramcontent.com/pod-product-compliance
Lightning Source LLC
Chambersburg PA
CBHW040748200526
45159CB00023B/1790